SAGE

Yaffa

All words copyright © 2025

All rights reserved.
Advanced Readers Copy
Published in 2025 by Meraj Publishing
1st Edition

Illustrations copyright © 2025
This is a work of creative nonfiction, poetry, and memoir. It reflects the author's present recollections of experiences over time. Some parts or names have been fictionalized in varying degrees, for various purposes.

No part of this book may be reproduced or used in any manner without written permission of the copyright owner except for the use of quotations in a book review. For more information, address:
info@merajpublishing.com

ISBN: 979-8-9925727-2-8 (Print)
ISBN: 979-8-9925727-4-2 (Ebook)

Cover by Yaffa AS

merajpublishing.com

Other publications by Yaffa:

Blood Orange
Inara: Light of Utopia
Desecrated Poppies
Whispers Beneath the Orange Grove
Living to 99
Letters from a Living Utopia

To the divine who are deemed too radiant to be free and are hunted, punished, and restricted—may you never forget that no cage can hold the infinite.

To Be	12
I Will Never	14
Ashamed	15
Eid	16
Cycle	17
Sounds of Home	18
Musical	19
Scared	21
To be Queer, Part 3	22
Blocka Blocka Blocka	24
Solitude	25
Forever Disposable	26
Soul	27
Heartbreak	29
20 Years Wasted	30
Wonder	31
Smile	32
Religion	33
Wonder Part 2	35
I'm Asked	36
Cool	38
Erase	39
Small	41
Sex	42
Weinkom Part 2	44
Life Differently	45
Untempered	47
Gaslighting	48
Pandoras Box	49

Mama	50
Gap	53
Resist	54
Loneliness	55
Murder	57
Right	58
Can't	59
Dispose of Me	60
Disowned	62
Died	63
Disown Family	64
I Hide	65
We're Talking About	66
Surreal	67
Hurt	69
I Don't Want	70
Un-	73
Ghosts	74
Death	75
Grief	77
Fine	78
How Dare You?	79
Wonder Part 3	80
Problem	83
Fine Part 2	85
My People Die Twice	86
Transitions	89
Visible?	90
Walking Home	94

Mama Doesn't Want Me to Die	97
Sam Nordquist	99
Imam Muhsin Hendricks	99
Fragile	101
Blood	103
Green	106
Rebirth	107
Transformation	109
Cancer New Moon	109
Bestsellers	112
Loss of Power	113
I Go Viral	116
Archive	117
Thin Line	118
Acknowledgments	120
About Meraj Publishing	121
About the Author	121

You cease fire
Not genocide

I am tired
of violence
from states
built to be violent
and from communities
who want to be
states themselves

To Be

I come before you
as someone who
has not been permitted
to be

you may wonder
Yaffa, how here
before us have you not been
permitted
to be?

if any of you
are able to shoot me down
for simply being
then am I permitted
to be?

I stand before you
not as the I of this body
I stand before you
as your children and grandchildren
the unhoused trans person
you pass by everyday
never asking their name or
who they want
to be

I come to you
not as a body
but as a soul
of countless beings
killed by your words
actions that you stood by

because it wasn't you
because you were permitted
to be

I stand before you
carrying thousands of
lives, not too different
than my own
but shot and killed
while I come before you
on my way
to be

I thrive
the knife on
my throat
and i feel it tearing
flesh everytime
one of me is not permitted
to be

I wish it was
me everytime
so I scream and write
talk louder
take up space
death threats galore
doxed and post stamped
waiting
to be

but I already am
yet I am killed
anyways forgetting
to be

I Will Never

pretend to be less
to satisfy whiteness
nor masculinity
nor femininity
nor able bodies
nor christianity
nor you

Ashamed

my family is ashamed
of my Transness
but they forget that they
have always been ashamed of
me
at every stage, at every
frame of my life
every school grade, every moment
they have been
ashamed

where do those of us
who have never had others be proud
go when our Transness is also
unacceptable?

I wonder, what place there is
for those of us who have never been truly liked
I wonder, what that does
to a person? when
everyone around you only likes you
when they do not know you?
when people step away and dislike you
as soon as they know you?

Eid

ringing bells and the smells
of maamoul
takbeerat in the distance
dancing to my heartbeat
my dress is gold and blue
purple and ruby
I am draped in silk and
embroidery
all the things at once and separately
capes and heels
summer hats in the winter
prayer gliding over sand dunes and hiking trails
by rivers and oceans
in forests of emerald and grace
embraces from regalia from every
corner of the world
at home and a tourist
wise and yearning to learn
I am balance
I am Eid

Cycle

I have a cycle
I miss them
I drop everything
be there
we fight
I hate them
again and again
where does it end?

I said, if someone
offered me 10 million
dollars to never talk to
them again, I'd do it
I would do it for half
even less
some days
most days

other days
they're priceless
and I am the only one
that pays

Sounds of Home

at a queer
Trans Muslim
Eid open mic
I find sounds
of creation
of mending my
already perfect soul
I find wings to float
held and supported

Musical

I used to dream
in music

every thought was filled
with poorly sang
ballads

every walk home
from school
every thoughtless moment
alone in my room
filled like a musical
a one person show

I never sang in public
I never seemed to understand
that those who made fun of my voice
were also drowning
in their own ways

I never remembered a single word
I sang
it was all in the moment
now I sing again
upset

It is Eid
It is dark

a little after midnight
B comes asking where I went
the song ends

we go home
to sleep
I dream
in silence

Scared

I am scared of the day
they tell me I can't be around
their kids
I am scared because it has already
happened, an inevitability

we are not the same
and I will be okay
like I have before and after
during and always
I have enough love
to love them anyways

To be Queer, Part 3

is to be
invisible, visible only
during full moons
solstices and astrological
convergence that you
might not understand

to be queer
is to be safe
within global majority
queer and Trans
spaces only — even then barely
recognizing all other
spaces are not

to be queer
is to know
you fuck with stars
even when you
don't understand
why gen Z says
'fuck with' so much

to be queer
is to know
that others are in
pain and they try
to blame you

to be queer
is to be objective
connected to the
Ajna chakra
without knowing
its name

to be queer
is to see yourself
for the first time
in Palestinian embroidery
at home in water

to be queer
is to be the sun
the moon, water
earth, lightning
and grace

to be queer
is to be
home
killed
in your sleep

Blocka Blocka Blocka

I yearn to only write
from a place of joy

but where do I put
the gaping wounds left behind

told I need to 'censor'
that the kids are growing

they don't want to answer
questions

their labor is more important
so I blocka blocka blocka

and
pretend to move on

Solitude

I love love love
being alone
my solitude my sanctuary
but when it hurts
when someone cuts
I want someone and
it's the only time
there's no one there

Forever Disposable

I said I'd give them
up for ten million dollars
didn't get the dollars

Soul

if I die
from a bullet
does my soul
get trapped within
the torn skin and bones
or does it leave before
the bullet strikes?

I ask
for friends
the dozens of forgotten
queer and Trans palestinians
in Gaza I mourn
and wonder where to find them

If I am the only one
carrying their names
am i the only one
who can call them?

what happens to their
names when my
soul joins them?

another massacre
at dawn, suhoor
beckoning
I cross the final name
of all I know and I
wonder if maybe
my list was in fact
a hit list or if my list just
fits into half a million

killed?

I wonder about
the next Trans muslim
child who dies from suicide
or killed by hands too white
to know that violence
is not love

will their soul
enter a gendered heaven?
a bird in the highest
levels of Janna,
or stuck between your politics
and dogma?
never realizing spirit
predates your politics

the bullets cuts
through me
you don't matter
now, you didn't matter
before, you will never matter
after

Heartbreak

it aches
in a way that
very little else
ever has
and I know
it is heartbreak

I cry on this plane
before we even take off
mask covering my snot
I can ugly cry here
in a sold out flight
as the person next to me
changes seats to be closer to
a loved one
they switch
another person
ignores my tears

20 Years Wasted

we are now a family
that will yearn twenty years
until your children have the sense
to seek me

we will cry
they will insist
it will still hurt

I will cry more
you will meet my child
for the first time

they will be grown
having never even heard of you

we will all cry
twenty years wasted
life lived

good bye forever I said
or at least twenty years

Wonder

some days I will wonder
how you are
I might even ask
my heart will bleed

I wonder if you'll read
these published words
if you'll weep too and
wonder about me

Smile

it's a smile
my greatest abandonment
gifted one day
withheld the next

Mama smiled once
Baba smiled once
T smiled
B smiled
F smiled
M smiled
C smiled
every sister
smiled

one day
there were no
more smiles
I fought back
resisted
begged for
the smiles to
return
in the only
ways I knew
pulling back
hiding
leaving
until the next
smiles
were taken

Religion

so you're saying
that because systemic
oppression has become
entrenched within religion
we should reject religion
instead of systemic oppression?

oh why not both?
you ask

honey, you're
barely doing one
let alone both...

I don't see you doing
both, I'm seeing you
doing one problematically

going around upholding
white supremacist narratives
about Indigenous folks spirituality
pretending as if your narratives
are any different from
the original imperialist
narratives calling
us savages, uncivilized, backwards
for everything that
you supposedly stand for
until it became our fabric too
and now you reject us
you reject yourself
because they still hurt us
now hurt us through you?

you tell me
the trans person
my faith is transphobic
you tell me
the queer person
my spirituality is queerphobic
you tell me
the femme person
my beliefs
are femmephobic
me? you?

the non-trans
non-queer
non-femme
person
you?
tell me?

honey, the fact you
think you can talk
to me in the first place
is white supremacist
boy bye!!!

Wonder Part 2

I wonder what your last
memory of me will be
what R's and H's memory
if any, will be

I wonder what you'll tell them
they will hear about me
from D and A and others
or at least until the other
sisters do the same

I lost you all last year
starting right after
Eid

am I bound to repeat
that this year?
this time with tears
of sorrow
instead of just anger and
malice?

I'm Asked

if I have names of
Trans Palestinians to add
to Trans day of remembrance

I struggle with an answer
knowing that the names I
know will never be uttered
fading even from my own memory

how do you ask
someone if they can
be added to a list
when their name is not
on ANY list

I am a death
worker, I ask the
hard questions about
death, but genocide is
not death

even then I ask
who to support after
who to follow up with
what their hopes and dreams
are

but they are not
anymore
Trans Palestinians do not
have the privilege of our
names on a list

I say knowing
that I'll have the privilege
of being on countless lists
when I am killed

Cool

you said
you were cool with things
but not around your kids
I wonder how many other
transphobes also think
they're cool

Erase

    you

                      want

        to erase

                                Me?

    ME?

          have you met me?

have you witnessed the earth shifting every time I take a step?

have you witnessed the stars fluttering in awe?

have you not seen the way the wind embraces my curls? the clouds hover in prayer? the sun shining in gratitude? or have you?

          remove the T
          remove the Q
          they weren't
          for you
          Anyways

question all
you like

honey, even 6
feet under

I breathe in land
stars welcoming me

>   there is no
>   universe that
>   forgets what
>   has always been
>   Divine

Small

I feel
small
as if flying
for the first
time, in the wild
unprotected
I'm not sure
why
maybe Taurus
season, maybe the
eclipses
maybe feeling
safe in my
one bedroom
overlooking San Pablo

NYC feels so large
scary with all
the people
who hurt
maybe it's
because I hurt
the last time I
left I lost
a sister
the outside is
loss and I
am in need of
protection

Sex

straight cis women
taught me the price
of accepting support
is sex, a relationship
and/or marriage

gay men taught me
a hand on a thigh
is consent

my neighbor taught
me sex is a game

my parents taught me
sex is wrong

my school taught me
sex is disrespectful

I learned
that I am wrong

and
I learned
sex is not an exchange
your tears are violent
there is no leading on
there is only consent
and there is no consent
to this body without
me

I am not a marriage
exchange
or a gift wrapped
for toy pianos
and a smile

you may keep
your support, your respect,
your ideas of love,
You may keep all of you

I'll be here
learning sex is magic
body-mind-spirit
bridging across constellations
trees of life
sprouting and rising
above all there is
and ever was
my thighs connecting
your ancestors with mine

you may keep
your sex
I'm here for life

Weinkom Part 2

I only want others
when I am so hurt it hurts
to breathe, to be

where are you?

Life Differently

I stare
into a camera
for hours
watching both
my parents aging
staring back
at me

my eyes slump
cheekbones askew
wrinkles crinkling
at the edges
sorrow in my
eyes
seeing this body and mine

they will die
I will die
together
alone

I am the strongest
person I will ever
truly know
I am also the weakest
malleable and flexible
growing infinitely
I am also the most tired
most everything

all I know
is me

they have known
each other
eight children
nine grandchildren and
counting
at my age they already
had 5 to 7 children
two wars behind
them

I am not lonely
yearning for a partner
and children
I am witnessing
life differently

Untempered

I have entered
anger
sheer raw untempered
no one is safe
my pain will be felt
everywhere
by everyone

air flows into
my right nostril
filling me with sun energy
as the moon is but a crescent
in the post Eid days
no one can hold a grudge
like a double Leo cancer
watch me

Gaslighting

am I overreacting?
dramatic?
I wonder how many
other Trans folks ask
themselves the same things?
families, friends, strangers
politicians and everyone else at
this point gaslighting us
into believing we are the
problem for not
'compromising'
'being more mindful
around their kids'

honey my existence
is a compromise
textiles can't capture
the fabrics that yearn to
drape this body
languages don't begin
to comprehend my voice
recognition of stardust
is a simplification that can't
begin to capture what stars are
or what I am

this is a compromise

Pandoras Box

Pandora met me once
unable to hold me she
cried, tears of everything I am
imprisoned me in a box
tossed me at sea
where I am Lost
never to be held again

oh how white women
make our pain about
them

Mama

I talk to mama
feel a breath of fresh
air entering my bones
I feel better
we're not perfect
but I don't hate myself
around her like I
do most sisters
suicidality does not beckon
after a few days

I'm grateful

Mama shares that
Baba dreamt that I
was at the Tasneem
a fountain in heaven
he thinks it means I'll
marry someone named
Tasneem
Mama thinks it means
I'm on the righteous path

I am blessed to
have them both
yet know our paths
are not the same
my heaven is their nightmare
no matter how much
they fear me and
pretend otherwise

I refuse to define

relationships by a spectrum
of transphobia

I remain in relationship
with mama
because she is
willing
not quite there yet
but willing to move

Even then,
I wonder hold long
a relationship built on
one sided growth and fear
can last?

Gap

tired of carrying the weight
of the between your
intentions & actions

Resist

my anger dissipates
my heart warms
I wonder if maybe we can
still be in relationship
maybe you can visit
maybe I can see you when
he's at work
maybe maybe
yet a part of me
resists the cycle

I am tired

Loneliness

the cold of loneliness
is upon me
between daisies and the greenest
blades of grass
between colossal gray
buildings
in San Francisco

it hurts in the same way
winter does
never enough layers or
too many
always itching to reach
my bones
always unwelcome

I sit on a sarong
back straight
sipping a too sweet
mint mojito coffee and
reading La Syrena

I yearn for touch
something safe and restful
meaning not human

I yearn to lay in warmth
with another body
that does not exist
to connect to this
borrowed body of mine
a stillness to my thoughts
a yearning to return

home after all
this time

I am lonely
after seeing a pile of shit
two blocks away
no one even blinks
I am lonely reading of home
waiting to see Scottsboro boys
I am lonely in a world
without sisters
without love nearby
it is hard to be the
source of love for everything

I wonder if the sun
yearns for another to also
shine so they may rest
someday her light will
recede and he will
die
never knowing rest until
then
why is death the only rest
we get in this life?

Murder

I have murdered
two males
in my life

the first the moment
I was born
Ayoub

the second my legal
cisness

my dad mourns
Ayoub

the rest mourn
their brother

I am left
an outsider
looking in

trying to replace
what was lost
only a shell of who
"I'm supposed to be"

Right

she says
we tell everyone
not to do certain
behaviors around
them and they
don't think we hate
them

I ask what
she'd say if I
told her she's
not allowed to
wear a scarf around
my kids

she says that's
different, it's religion
I say no, it's identity

I ask why it
matters if I ever
see her kids again
she doesn't answer

I say that's
her right as a
parent

I hang up

Can't

why can't
we talk about this
you say

why can't we
I wonder
why can't we

Dispose of Me

will you not?
my badge of
honour
a people who
only know to cannibalize
themselves
one after the other
when threatened by
systems that
lead to extinction

dispose of me
will you?
for I am terror
an ist
you shake at
my birth name
and quiver
in disgust at
transness that
was never
for you

dispose
you?
we are not
the same
disposing of you
grants you
bestsellers and
awards
But me?
I lose everything

you said was
important

dispose of me
please
it's all you can
be good for

I will always
gain myself

Disowned

I don't want
to be another
disowned
child

I don't want
that to be
my story
but is it not
already?

Died

it feels like
I have died
at least is that not
what they all think?
the thousands of people
who knew me under a different name
different clothes, maybe even a
different voice
those who knew and now mourn
cisness
I have died
reborn into something else
something more

Disown Family

am I an only child
if I disown my sisters?
did I disown them
or did they disown me?
who disowns who?
when they are transphobic
and I am Trans
refusing

I Hide

sun
bathing in the
30MPH winds
waiting for the
storm

Mama says
I've never seen you
laughing or maybe
she says I haven't seen you
laugh in a long time
I say I laugh all
the time
just never around
family

I don't think it's the
latter because I can't
remember laughing around
her either
not ever, not now
so I step out
to the sun
awaiting the
storm that's
already here

We're Talking About

Trans kids dying from
suicide
Mama says you
"look skinny are
you not eating?"

Surreal

it feels far away
surreal even
the situation and you
as if we haven't talked
in years
like we weren't bonded
by blood

hmmm weren't
weren't

I didn't expect
it'd feel so distant
so fast

it's been a day and a half
it feels like
you were evicted
from my heart
even your shadow
gone

yet I'm up
near 1 AM
thinking of you
me, your babies, and
the trash you call a
husband

I don't have
the best of memories
soon I may forget
you, them, us

entirely
I wonder if you'll
know, and if
you'll forget too

I wonder if
I'm also surreal
to you

Hurt

days pass
I'm not sure
how
many, less
than a week
you don't try
to contact me
we were on a family
call together, briefly
I could feel your hurt
I wished transphobes
wouldn't hurt
because you hurt

Y-o-u h-u-r-t

I Don't Want

your
"I'm thinking of yous"
"thoughts and
prayers"
unnerve me
and I wonder
to what God are you
praying?
mine or yours?
when yours is
white supremacy and
mine still loves
the human deep
deep, deep, within

you — just heard plans
we've been telling you
about for
lifetimes
wondering
How
I
am?
lol

you blame trump
for what you
voted for
told me this is on
me
made me videos
of you eating popcorn
watching my family incinerated

you at Starbucks drinking
as if genocide was a too
sweet drink
too overpriced
busting unions
with every
sip

I don't want
your thoughts
your prayers
your condolences
sympathies
empathies
compassions
as if bombs fall from
the sky due to climate change
unnaturally natural
'nothing to be done'
because your God willed
it and mine told me
you're not worth
the violence

I type on a
new iPhone
that someone's child
died to make
wishing that when
the bombs rain
I'm home and no
where near
whatever hell
you live in
to send thoughts and

prayers

twenty years
from now you'll
say you remember
today
none of us around
to counter
your narrative of
saviorhood
even Jesus was blessed
with whiteness
300 years later

as if we didn't
tell you this
ends in
flame

I'm thinking of
you too
sending you
thoughts and prayers
may you always stay hydrated

Un-

we're all going
to die someday
holding onto so
many truths
loss untold
hugs ungiven
breathes unshared
embraces unloved
life unlived

I'm going
to die someday
still yearning for
a hug from
Mama
Baba
every sister
unrequited love
unlaced with immense
pain

Ghosts

in a car
on the way to
embroidery and home
you said your religion
does not include my
existence but that does not
mean you love me less

you admitted you hold onto
a brother who died
angry that I say such things
he is real to you
you say and I say he is
to you and not to me
so what are we?

What are we
when I do not exist
a relationship with a ghost
denied is not a relationship
I seek – for I have
my own ghosts to please
and you
are not one of them

Death

if death
were a person
they – yes they
for who else but the
genderqueer can move
beyond space and time
to create life without life

they – would ask
to be comforted
from the weight of
being what they are
knowing self-sufficiency
is injustice carried
alone

they – would be
told they are not real
a slice of time and space
unable to be defined
without life

they – would
wonder if they were not
life who has lost
her will and charm

they – would carry
the souls passing through
guiding him as he kicks
and screams
saying the worst of things
only to grow at the end

never looking back
never acknowledging their
labor

they – would be me
moving between realms
and lives
knowing death and life
are not a binary

they – are an
existence beyond
binaries
siblings to life
sorrow, wisdom, queerness
superiority, envy
shame

they – encompass all
yet are none
but a simple guide
beyond

if life were reason
death is wonder
and they are not
mutually exclusive

Grief

others share pain
frustration, mostly grief
navigating queer and trans
Muslim identity
folks who love us
despise what we are
often pretending otherwise
speaking of boundaries and
respect

in reality saying:

> I will tell my children
> YOU are wrong

with terror in your eyes

am I the worst
your children can be?

Fine

you ask,
"how are u?
are you still thinking?
or is everything good?"

I reply, everything is fine.

goodbye

How Dare You?

say that we just
won't talk about it
"a *difference* of opinion
doesn't need to
tear us apart"
as if
Trans kids
aren't dying
as if your governments
aren't cutting
my circulation
why would I
step into any room
where you think
it's okay to not even
try to get it
try to see
yourself as the
murderer?

Wonder Part 3

I wonder what
It's like
to not be told
that you are not
enough
to not be told that
you are an anomaly
all the magic you bring
an error
I wonder what it's like
to be supported and validated
from the start
not just the end

I wonder what it's
like to not have to fight
for everything and anything
those you fought claiming
credit for every success

I wonder
I don't necessarily want
that
I just wonder
I cradle my heart
between languages
torn and demanded
yearning to be spoken and
forgotten
like me
between the loneliness
and yearning there is
space to exist beyond

ego
I dive into it
a pool of finely
embroidered fabric
no start no end
only being

this Eid
I teleport to beaches
where I can be naked
reading QTM words
anklets clinging and the
bracelet I made connecting
me to what is above
and below as I
hover in the in-between
inhaling the ocean
exhaling the cosmos
my body melting
mind warping as if
lost within mushrooms

I am sober but
what is sobriety when
all drugs grant
temporary entrance into
the fabrics that you
already live on?

last year I searched
for stones that would
allow the universe to
go through me
feeling its pressure building
against the hole of my soul

never relaxed enough to
be penetrated
now I know that bodies
must prep for years
decades sometimes
to be ready to receive
I am filled temporarily
preparing for more

what do you do
during conflict with
an actively dying person?
does it make it any
better when they dehumanize
you along the way?
because soon they'll die?
that sounds far worse
than walking towards
accountability with
them

I wonder if
our hatred for supremacy
will ever surpass our hatred of
accountability

Problem

am I the problem?
I ask myself again and again
for decades
knowing that there is never
a single problem just
wounds of being that
prick one another

they say
I have seen you turn
off every relationship
you have
a lie and yet
it circles my mind
a sun headache pressuring
my forehead begging
for release or
something I'm not sure
what

am I the problem
when I am the disposable
one?
she says we didn't mean
it that way
why do you take it
this way?
another's cancer metastasized
I am an unpaid caregiver
begging for connection
giving it all up
another lies, asks for
labor that is not rightfully

hers

the right name
the pronouns
the work
all of it not
honored
I am
not honored

am I the problem?
a Leo/Cancer begging
for attention and love
I must be
when everyone has left
again and again

then, I remind myself
that these societies are
white supremacist and
Transmisic and so much
more

am I the problem?
or is being everything
I am the problem?

either way
I am the problem

Fine Part 2

one month later
my insides still twist
as if held and powdered
again and again
we have not talked
your calls go unanswered
I pretend I am fine
awake at 4AM thinking
unsure what else
to do
stuck between letting go
and lost on the way
home

My People Die Twice

they talk about
pink washing
yet throw my book
saying we don't do
that here

they talk about
pink washing
a 76 org
coalition torn apart
at the mention
of my name

they talk about
pink washing
encampment torn
to shreds at
the mention of
me

somehow
my transness
has become a
threat to everything
Falasteen

she says
I told them only
Yaffa works with
Queer and Trans Palestinians
I say I know
I wonder why a
year and a half into

this it's still only
me

they say
we can't let them
weaponize transphobia
within our communities
against us
honey, they already
have, already
do

she asks if
it's okay to connect
Trans Syrians to
them and I have
to be the one to
say no
they're transphobic

he calls me a
cult leader
FBI informant
can't be Muslim and Trans

she yells, top
of her lungs
says I messed up
says she doesn't want to
get stuck between
me and everyone coming
after me
I lose another friend
she wonders why

he asks if
we can date
I wonder who
he's asking
Misgendered
shattered pieces
between two hammers
neither look like
me

my people die
twice

Transitions

they ask about
transitioning
the first doctor to
ask on their own

I don't know how
to explain to them
that not all of us
get to transition

sometimes
those of us
at the intersections of
immigration, disability,
displacement, deportation
and ongoing
genocide
do not get to
transition

transitions are hard
for everyone
for some of us
they are a death
sentence

even then,
they do not fully understand
not knowing that it is
what we hide
that sometimes
keeps us alive

Visible?

visible?
to be Trans and visible
is to welcome death

best of cases
it's the death of
a cis parasite that
forced their way
into your body
claiming it for its own
society celebrating it as you
fall under excruciating
pain

worst of cases
you are erased
murdered, disappeared
kidnapped
murdered the best of these
options

ICE knocks on doors
friends video the trafficking
lawyers search between state lines
moved again and again
but I can't remember
the last time someone walked
me home to film
or call a lawyer
or search

I am visible
so visible that entire communities

tear each other apart
my makeup
glittered in night skies
that forgot there were
stars above
beyond
the satellites

I disappear
it takes weeks for anyone
other than mama to
notice
she expects me to cut
her off any day now
she and so many others
will assume I have cut
them out because of
their transphobia

dozens of Trans
people have disappeared
around me over the years
I hold hope they are
home, wherever home
is, knowing that phones and
emails will not
save us

I hold hope
I know we are disappeared
everyday, invisible
visible only in their
imaginations

TDOV

and I wonder
if it's actually just doves
raining down
bloodied and bruised
ready for the next
world

I am tired
of visibility and
invisibility
my body scarred
my mind pulled
my soul sullied
barred from heaven
when heaven is our
only home

D asks how zionists
can kill us as if
it's nothing
I say you won't
call me by my name
knowing how much it
hurts
she says nothing
I want to scream
into the voids
between all my
peoples

I don't know
who to mourn
anymore
when all my
peoples are killed

and I don't know
where to find them
bodies scattered between
mines, minds scattered
between pills, souls
scattered between
satellites, lost
between stars

I hold hope
stars calling us
home
one way or another
fascism may detour
our return but
return we shall

Walking Home

grief opens my
heart
I understand
I know
I really do

you couldn't
be there
when the world
didn't have
space for you
too

there is sadness
and profound joy
my 31st birthday
moving me into
32 years
on this planet
in this vessel

my joy knows
no bounds
friends' spirits
filling my world
with gifts and
wishes that
carry me

there is sadness
at being alone
today

some who were
loved ones
forgetting me
and all that I am

the cryo did not
freeze the parts
that are still trying
to hang on
the infrared sauna
cleansing me
from the inside
I float
joyful

carrying
the weight
of all emotions
that amplify
joy

if I lose
my words
what will be
left?

those of us
with disability
that lose words
memories, and images
ask ourselves often
at least, I do

if I lose
the parts

that are valued
who will carry me?

sometimes I think
the only reason
there's anything left
of me is because
there's no one
to pick up the
pieces

I suppose
everyone
feels that way
do they not?

the universe
will always catch
what's left of us
and take the rest
home

one day
I will return
home
disability
ability
none matter

Mama Doesn't Want Me to Die

so she doesn't want me
to be trans

she knows trans
is lethal

she knows she's
right
I know
she's not
wrong

I will be
killed for being trans
not 🍉
not disability
not Muslim
not immigrant

but Trans

Trans kills
they all kill
Trans means
no Muslim burial
Trans means
erased from Falasteen
Trans means
no one to fight
for me

Mama knows
because she doesn't
fight for Trans

Trans dies
she doesn't want
me to die

Sam Nordquist
Imam Muhsin Hendricks

hours apart
days between them
thousand of miles
rarely mentioned together

both killed
both gone
both erased
only us naming

naming
naming
naming
forgetting names
disassociating
nervous systems nervous

are we nervous?
am I nervous on this train from NYC?

Kuffiyeh like a crown
earrings like royal jewels
Trans-Muslim-Fabulous on my shirt

I wonder what's left of me when they keep killing me everywhere

I wonder what's left when half my people believe the death of the rest of me is invalid

Mama asks
"why can't you just see them?"

I tell her about Sam but with a different name.
so many names.
I forget my own.

will they know to remember a name I've forgotten?
I hope they don't

my name will not be strategically uttered
another name is just another name they forget or worse ignore

may they remember something they can't ignore
may they remember something that triggers a revolution
where we don't have names

may the nameless,
rise

may the named,
rest

Fragile

your neck spasms
like mine did last
year

losing loved ones
can kill

I wonder if this will
snap your neck

we're such fragile
beings

any of us can be
gone any moment

yet you insist you're
never wrong

the weight of lives
is far too
large of a burden
to carry

you wonder why
I can't talk to you
I almost do sometimes
then I get the next call
text, or worse nothing
at all

I see your eyes
everytime a trans child

is killed

I hear your voice
everytime zionists
tell me they're saving
my life
while killing every queer and
Trans person I know
in Gaza

if you've said
the same words
they have, does
it really matter if
you weren't the
one pulling the
trigger?

call me naive
call me idealistic
call me whatever you
want

I still get the calls
I still wonder if
I'll ever hear from them
again

I'm still the one
who will be
killed
misgendered post-mortem
while people like you
say it was never
their fault

Blood

do we share the
same blood?

when we've never
eaten from the
same land

never inhaled the
same air

when your blood
is spilled and
I beg for blood tests
in a land without
healthcare?

are we of
the same blood
when my bones are
raw from too many
planes while you dream
of flight?

are we of
the same blood
when mine will be
partially considered
while yours is erased?

are we of
the same blood
when they point
guns at me

for every ditch
my car finds?

are we of
the same blood
when you can't
leave your borders
and I am deported
from all mine?

are we of
the same blood
when they call me
a savage, rapist, murderer?

are we of
the same blood
when we're not
buried, desecrated, erased
only our land remembering?

are we of
the same blood
when I've lost all
my family and you've
lost all yours?

are we of
the same blood
when yours were murdered due
to white supremacy and
mine lost who they are?

she says
you look like them

your moms family
while everyone else
asks
are we of
the same blood?

Green

these poems
are titled green
others were purple
titled in colors that mean
everything and nothing
I didn't know
they'd be green
at the start
I wonder if pain
is now green
it was meant
for joy
joy needs to wait
until systems are
detoxed, expunged, if
that's a real
word
I'm tired
wearing green
on my way
to acupuncture
thinking of sisters
hoping needles will
expel you all

Rebirth

I go in and out
checking in with
organs, needles piercing
over a dozen points
on my skin
working to cleanse me
of sisters and allergies
that try to destroy
everything I am
mostly unintentionally

after an hour
I rise above
to the Sagittarius
full moon
I say hello
to the fire of the sun
and the fire of the moon
I am quickly enveloped in
warm flames
feelings of belonging and
home remembered
butterfly wings
like a fairy's spark to life
I wonder about dragons and
one forms beside me
he guides and protects
but is not me

for hours I am
cradled by the
two halves of the
moon

they embrace me
and as they release,
the fire from my wings
circles around me
creating an egg shape
a womb
the one that started
last month
during Scorpio full moon
I know immediately that
this is the second of four
transformations
I must shelter in fire
to harden into lava rock
to be torn apart
and rise anew
I am rebirthing

Transformation
Cancer New Moon

I think about
hearts closing
only to open in
other ways

how when something
turns to stone
it's molecules
become something
else entirely

as it shatters
air tearing away
water cutting through
or remade by fire
it awakens
open and whole
a different being

cycles of closing
our hearts are
transformative

rage, hate
every emotion
we are told to
move away from
transforms

everything
moves us to
transformation

except for
our denial
of transformations
constance

Joy

the wheatgrass reflects the late afternoon sun
just peeking through the hills to the west.

I run,
gravity and the sloping ground increasing my speed
until I'm not sure if I can stop myself.
I don't.

The sun's rays head home,
one by one,

I look down to find that I had peed myself.
There is no warmth, no marks.

Fear hits me, like the wind pushing the wheat towards itself.

I am now an adult, I smile again,
I'd pee every time if it meant being home.

Another child, now an adult pees in grass
Someone notices, hugs them as they cry, changes them,
and they run back.

The field is left, developing love, concrete left behind.
without roofs or metallic wires.

A time loop, countless children experiencing joy for the first time.

Bestsellers

I don't write
to make it on
bestseller lists
or even for you
to read these words
today

I write and publish
because some day
someone is going to
need them

someday post mortem
they will become more
accessible

someday you
will read these words,
you may not know who
I am but I
will have served my
purpose

I will have published words
from countless generations
spirits much greater
than I

These words
recycled into
universal consciousness
never lost

Loss of Power

he clings to
the car door
as I drive away
his shoes scraping
the pavement
begging me to
come inside
to talk it out

a part of it is
sweet
the other – where
my nervous system
is on fire
wonders if I'll
ever be free

she joins him
a baby in tow
and I wonder
if I'm wrong
if I can't just
...
he says
they're compromising
by overlooking this
behavior and still
accepting me
he says they love
me
and wonders if I've
considered how hard
that is for them

if I appreciate anything
at all

...

he says
he won't let A
visit next week.
he's lost
grasping at straws
loss is real
for him
too

...

he says
they'll "accept me
positively
for everything
I am"
the right name
right whatever
and I wonder
why it always
takes me fighting
to get here

...

he says
this is the last
goodbye
I say it is

...

they say
I have watched you
turn on and off
every relationship

...

maybe it's time

for a complete
loss of
power

I Go Viral

every time someone
is killed
as if that's a
consolation
of some kind

as if
posting matters
more

I wish you never
knew My name

maybe then
no one would
have died

Archive

someday
the biggest
global majority
Trans archive will be
public

it'll just be
FBI files about us

it'll be extensive
profound
so many of us
will finally
be seen

Thin Line

it's a thin
line between
life and death
post surgery

infections bleeding into
fever, feeding ulcers
as I wait
ten days back and
forth between worlds

I realize I hate who I am
around my family because
they don't believe in the
best parts
surgically cutting queerness and
Transness, even my autism
erased

I sleep on the couch
a dozen nights
a shell so empty
I wonder if they see me
lying here at all

they bring me all the
things I hate
the things I do not
need
I realize finally
I'm not here
at all

never invited
never embraced

a ghost hovers
memories that never were
a time capsule
of someone else

Acknowledgments

This collection was written over a longer period of time than many of my more recent publications, starting in March 2023. Which means that the individuals who witnessed me at the start are not necessarily the individuals who are in my life today. October 7th, 2023 cut through this book and with that a lot of loss of friends, family, and trans individuals in my life. Relationships changed —- the dozens of queer and trans people I knew in Gaza before Oct 7th have been killed in a world that does not acknowledge their existence even as they fight for them as Palestinian. The world is different, like it is every day. I am grateful to the people from the before times and the after — whenever you end up reading this work. Since there are more names I am unable to name here than the names I can I choose to not name anyone. Know that I am grateful, whatever role you have played in my journey throughout these years, no matter how small or large, whether you have been harmful or kind or both. I am grateful for it all.

To those I am unable to name, may we build a world where you may be named but never have to be.

About Meraj Publishing

Meraj Publishing is a Trans and Queer Muslim publishing house that centers TQM voices from the global majority, with a focus on Palestinian and Black Authors. Recognizing the vast inequities in the publishing industry, we aim to enable TQM individuals from the global majority to fully own our stories. Meraj prioritizes stories that focus on building utopia, hope, love, spirituality, and belonging. Meraj Publishing is entirely run and operated by the TQM global majority.

About the Author

Photo by Michael Colgan

Yaffa (they/them) is a stand-up comedian currently withholding their comedy until Falasteen is free. In the meantime, they have vowed to flood the market with books, visual art, and perhaps even plays.

They are an acclaimed disabled, autistic, trans, queer, Muslim, Indigenous Palestinian. Mx. Yaffa is the Executive Director of the Muslim Alliance for Sexual and Gender Diversity (MASGD) and the founder of several non-profits and community projects.

They are multi-generationally displaced and currently searching for the next country to move to. They currently split their time between Jordan and Occupied Lisjan territory, where they are in service to Indigenous communities until they can return home to Falasteen.

www.ingramcontent.com/pod-product-compliance
Lightning Source LLC
Chambersburg PA
CBHW070548090426
42735CB00013B/3106